C000165476

Honey Tree Publishing
www.honeytreepublishingus.com

Hostile Takeover: A Systematic and Psychological Manifestation of a Cultural Reality

First Paperback Edition 2023

For more information or to process a book order, please visit www.duanecampbell.com or email Duane Campbell at iamtheglow@hotmail.com

Manufactured in the United States of America

ISBN: 979-8-9878336-1-2

OTHER BOOKS BY THE AUTHOR

Perpetual Domain (Volume One of The Awareness Project) Doghouse Publishing (1994)

Inner Strength Defies the Skeptic (A Psychological and Spiritual Guide from Fear to Freedom) Immediex Publishing (2006)

From Preschool to the Penitentiary (A Candid Examination of a Vicious Cycle) African American Images Publishing (2015)

DEDICATION

this body of work, and all else that i do, is dedicated to the arrogant and egotistical underestimations of us; that we may transcend beyond the influence of negative ideologies...

and of the intrinsic genius dwelling within each of us; that would challenge the most basic commonality of an oftentimes conceded and inferior concept that dominates the minds and behaviors of humanistic endeavor...

to the loneliness that forces the honesty of thought and is translated through the quietness and unspoken curiosity of my own meditation...

and to the genuine ways of those who by your kindness and unselfish acts of love; would make he who sometimes feels to be the outcast and all alone; the thirsting and most willing recipient of your sincere and welcoming embrace...

WeR1...

Duane Campbell

PREFACE

Hostile Takeover: A Systematic and Psychological Manifestation of a Cultural Reality illustrates the presence of racism in America and its contribution to the self-degradation and inferiority complex experienced by many Black people in America. This book explores how racism is a source of manipulation and control across social systems, such as politics, education, healthcare, and community development. This book aims to introduce new verbiage in the old lexicon of how systemic racism has impacted the Black psyche, thus extending deeply into the reality of our human condition.

Within this book, you will find countless examples of the spiritual and psychological wages of war that have successfully subjugated the potential of an entire human population. White supremacists, racist profiteers, provide the perverse arsenals of war that sustain environmental self-destruction by way of a violent drug culture that fronts as a supplemental job market within the Black community, enhancing a volatile atmosphere of cultural eradication. Manipulation leads to a racial hierarchy of perceived achievement and success in America, as the rules of engagement favor White supremacy, often yielding devastating results for the Black collective.

This strategic initiative specifically examines the subtle tactics of warfare and its generational outreach. The indelible scar from this war not only marks the tortured memories of the existing but the unborn souls of those who have yet to arrive.

Dear reader, I hope that you read this book "cautiously" as it was written with "cautious intent" to make plain the complex and prevailing conditions of our dilemma.

Hostile Takeover is an ambitious endeavor, directly challenging the oppressive and traumatic conditions that have historically stifled the cultural progression of the Black collective. Within this dialectic, frustration and rage derived from the captivity of psychological and spiritual control reaches into the subconscious mindset of emotionally transfixed people by the physical and sociological struggles of unimaginable torment and oppression. Thus, *Hostile Takeover* may possess some interpretive complexities for the reader.

***

There is a paradigm shift that seeks to rearrange the acquisitions of information influencing intellectual consciousness. This catalyst resides within those who step outside the proverbial box consisting of political, sociological, and psychological constructs consistent with a White supremacist ideology.

Essentially, stepping outside the proverbial box tests the oppressive social boundaries of intellectual critique and perspectives that lend themselves to liberatory existence as a strenuous concern of the contemptuous hierarchy of White supremacy.

New schools of progressive thinking challenge racism, and there is a growing resistance to the aforementioned ideologies. Independent thoughts and decisions create new pathways and avenues of curiosity for philosophical understanding leading to practicality. These pathways to cultural conditioning are either to the betterment or the detriment of the collective. Racism enacted in the prison

industrial complex, economic deprivation, health inequities, and educational disparities ultimately suppress the aspirations of the Black collective.

Oxford Languages, and dictionaries alike, define "Psychological" as "affecting or arising in the mind; related to the mental and emotional state of a person." This definition considers how the effects of environmental and behavioral conditions can influence one's state of mind, including emotional stability. Globally, there is a conscious effort to interject into the thought process of false narratives and perceptions that compromise the true cultural reality of Black people. Historically, this type of misconstrued portrait of Black culture has plagued all Black people, especially in the negative portrayal of Black men with racial stereotypes.

Charles Darwin, a racist geologist, and naturalist shared his theory that positioned the White race as the apex of human evolution. This theory was introduced in his book, "On the Origin of Species by Means of Natural Selection, or the Preservation of Favoured Races in the Struggle for Life" (1859). Scientific research influenced all areas of American culture, including American cinema. D.W. Griffiths "The Birth of a Nation" (1915), the first picture film produced in America, promoted racist themes and inaccurately depicted Black people as subhuman, hypersexualized, and uneducated savages. As a result, the media further marketed inaccurate stereotypes of Black people, such as Black men's lust for white women, justifying lynching.

Furthermore, the psychological impact of racism on Black people has been examined in research-based studies such as the "Doll Test," developed by Psychologists Kenneth and Mamie Clark in the late 1930s and 1940s. The "Doll Test" invented by psychologists Kenneth and Mamie Clark, was conducted in the late 1930s and 1940s to test children's understanding of race using two dolls, one Black and one White. The study found a vast majority of the children, both Black and White, when asked a series of questions, such as: Which doll is the most attractive or desirable? Which doll is the good doll? Which doll is the bad doll? The responses from the two racially different groups of children were reflective of the impact of racism. The White doll was selected as most desirable among the White children and most of the Black children. Whereas the Black doll was selected as the bad doll by an overwhelming majority of White and Black children. When questioned as to which doll was most likened to themselves, the Black children chose the Black doll, and the White children chose the White doll.

The spiritual and psychological reprogramming of Black people has altered and weakened our self-perceptions administered by White racists who stand at genocidal gates that contribute to the inferiority complex and self-loathing commonly associated with Black people to this day.

These ideological and behavioral influences impact the Black family and its generational legacy extending to our ancestral greatness that raised the great pyramids of Egypt. However, historically, we have been systematically severed since being made a slave, burned alive, dismembered, raped, lynched, a test subject of Eugenics and the Tuskegee experiments, miseducated, and victimized by the criminal justice system. These tactics have successfully reprogrammed the psyche of Black people on a cultural and conscious level. As a result, we must examine two types of cross-cultural warfare in society. First, physical warfare encompasses violent altercations resulting in the destruction of property and the loss of life. Second, sociological warfare struggles to disrupt and reassess the current conditions of the American status quo. Both types of warfare are designed to consider the eradication of White supremacy. We must be conscious and diligent of the premises and aspects of warfare.

Post-Traumatic Stress Disorder (PTSD) manifests itself in the idiosyncrasies of Black people which lends itself to "Learned Helplessness" within the subconscious psyche. This connection speaks to the balances and imbalances of war and peace. Black contemplation considers the directional probabilities of war and peace. This contemplation is interjected into the rhetorical arena of social injustice and inequality, yielding no relief or presumption of transcendence from our condition. Engaging in this taxing inner conflict creates anguish, smothering the biblical "eye for an eye," which is a disturbing concept essential to examining passive-aggressive ideology and combating the unabashed volatility of White supremacy. Ultimately, White supremacy pervades the developmental matrix of Black cultural consciousness and distorts the elemental fabric that sustains spiritual continuity and psychological self-preservation.

The foundational and actual working mechanisms that congest and complicate our structural and ideological perceptions are profoundly intricate within any attempt at a defined explanation that continues to baffle the ponderous search and discovery of our overall elevation.

The perplexing structural entanglement relative to the systematic and psychological conditions adversely responds to the oppressed masses. Confronting this issue complicates the foundational influences that would decisively impact the evolutionary progression of sociological interaction, which is essential to the imminent demise of White supremacy.

Business, housing, and education are primary examples of essential applications to be considered and interjected into the mainframe of revolutionary thought and action as they progressively influence cultural and sociological elevations that are vital elements to the developing consciousness of the oppressed and subjugated. The progressive mechanics of both types of elevation and their sequential significance are essential on a mental and emotional level to disturb those perceptive outcomes of individual and collective dilemmas. Addressing this psychological "conflict of interest" proves divisive to the unification of the oppressed masses that has strategically become an alternate reality.

In my previous book, "From Preschool to the Penitentiary (A Candid Examination of a Vicious

9

Cycle) published in 2015, I speak in candid detail on the subject of "Black Flight" and its developmental effects concerning the structural empowerment of the Black community and the reality of socioeconomic ascension. The segmented divisions of Black social reality are a tactical design, inciting cultural confrontation to instill and maintain a perpetual inner conflict within the construct of Black unity and productive development. Within this confused perceptive mindset of the Black collective, the ironic "us" versus "them" mentality is literally "us," meaning "Black people" against "them," meaning "Black people.

To contemplate our demise, confirming a sick ideology of self-hatred that validates our spiritual and psychological condition, skews perception. While White supremacy should exist to us as a developmental non-factor, tactically non-essential to our plight, our subconscious rejection of fear remains suppressed, which is most concerning and disturbing of our formative reality.

There is an element of self-determination that carries a mantle of responsibility to motivate the positive elevation of our culture. It exists within us as an obligation to inspire and influence others to build upon and safeguard the foundational structures that are catalysts to the subconscious and conscious eradication of White supremacy. This book depicts the cornerstones of our legacy reflected through a prism of spiritual paganism leading to psychological dissonance obstructing our true sense of self. This spiritual and psychological disconnection achieves the pervasive objectives of White supremacy, sustaining the status quo of the White elite and Black cultural underclass.

Racism is a psychological strategy that successfully maintains Black oppression. This psychological manipulation leads to spiritual oppression modifying Black values– spiritual and cultural– compromising Black elevation. For example, racists enact laws designed to minimize the unified structure of the Black family which negatively impacts Black cultural development. Society has proven that these living conditions are created from the "survival of the fittest" paradigm-shifting us from the basic elements of compassion and community building. This cultural dissonance leads to a conditioned mindset conducive to the insidious plan of White supremacists or racists.

In the context of this book, both are synonymous as they contribute to the same debilitating reality for many Black people. White supremacy is only successful through its ability to sustain psychological, sociological, and environmental control that contributes to the most traumatic circumstances of the Black condition compromising Black unity and leading to a disturbing cultural norm revealing itself through self-hatred and self-deprivation, perpetually infectious to the higher aspirations of an entire culture. Consequently, we must seek an understanding of this phenomenon that obstructs our generational elevation.

Historically, Black people have been negatively portrayed through a racist lens. American media where conflicting messages re-produce racist stereotypes and cultural misunderstandings of

Black culture and consciousness is a prime example of how racist stereotypes of Black people are reproduced for the benefit of White supremacists and to the detriment of Black cultural elevation. Mass media– music, film, advertisements, and the news– perpetuates the racist doctrine of Black cultural inferiority. The twisted irony of the racist segregationist suggests that Black people were and are unfit to co-exist with White America.

The manipulation of power to distort the reality of racial and cultural perception on a global scale is indicative of yet another false-positive illusion of Black cultural development and actuality. The effects of this intentional distortion pervade our cognitive processes. Black women are often portrayed as angry and hypersexualized, whereas,

Black men are portrayed as dope dealers, pimps, dead-beat parents, gang bangers, and killers.

Subliminal messages are also present in advertisements. The subliminal twist from good to evil displays the clever misdirection of the cultural mindset. The not-so-innocent "Angel Food Cake" (White cake) and "Devil's Food Cake" (Chocolate cake) analogies have defined their psychologically egregious intent. The infliction is indiscriminate. Generationally, the White cultural mindset instills yet another falsity to further influence fear and inferiority in the Black cultural mindset.

The "White is good" and "Black is evil" concept is a psychological trigger that induces the reactionary responses of self-loathing and cultural defamation that detrimentally inhibits the elevation of racial and social mobility. The psychologically conditioned Black lesser self, through a process of reevaluation, conforms to social events that play out in real-time.

The media successfully creates a toxic universal representation of Black people through the lens of racists. This portrayal is not reflective of divine greatness. With this understanding, we must examine the origin of human life, including the foundation of the Black family from a conscious mindset or perspective to challenge racism and its psychological impact, especially as it relates to the media.

Racists created and implemented advertisements to market catastrophic social events of the day, such as "picnics" derived from the term, "pick-a-nigger." This advertised climatic event consisted of torture, castration, burning alive, lynching, and the dismemberment of Black men, women, and children, to the delight and utter satisfaction of a predominately White crowd. Some Black people, sanctioned by White citizens, were made to witness the event that further engrained the horrific conditions of Black reality in America into Black consciousness. Many White participants in this horrific "festivity" sold the dismembered body parts of their victims to other Whites as personal keepsakes and family souvenirs. Black babies were also tossed into the murky southern swamps as alligator bait to demonstrate the perverse and sociopathic intentions of racists. These terrifying atrocities are imposed upon an entire culture and continue to evolve.

Today, racist stereotypes in the media negatively shape the realities of Black people on a variety of levels. Black people lie dying in the streets, murdered by the vicious and deadly judgment of law enforcement race soldiers or territorial street violence among their kind. The race-based execution of Black people by modern-day "slave catchers" with 21st-century "convict leasing" of predominantly Black men through the oxymoronic criminal justice system demonstrates the stark reality of the Black experience in America. This tactic assures predetermined quotas to sustain optimal levels of "mass incarceration" in compliance with a racist agenda that epitomizes new methods of slavery as the prison industrial complex expands upon its racist agenda of economic and social engineering. The racist and ill-equipped educational system impedes children's mental and behavioral potential, not to mention the prescription of psychotropic drugs as one of many variables leading to mass incarceration.

Furthermore, Black people are victims of drug-infested warzones representing a supplemental job market designed for America's Black inner-city communities– realities that both promote and fulfill a perpetual cycle of self-destruction. Furthermore, cultural manipulation of the Black business district effectively blocks the Black community's upward mobility. Black men are often relegated to the demeaning task of picking up trash in the parking lot and soliciting tips from the White, Asian, Jewish, and Arab business owners. These businesspersons control the cash registers and collect dollars from impoverished Black families with no consideration for Black community reinvestment.

Poverty and oppression negatively influence Black cultural development leading to sociological and psychological inferiority. It is no surprise that the American political strategy has effectively proposed and enacted legislation to directly impact the cohesiveness of the Black family structure, as most evident in governmental and public housing, healthcare, education, the criminal justice system, and employment. Government-controlled institutions produce vicious cycles of divisiveness, impacting the emotional and spiritual bond between the Black man and the Black woman. This dissension leads to stressors of pride, leadership, and the basic human survival instincts that jeopardize the stability of the Black family. As a result, this conflict is sustained through successful racist tactics to keep Black people forever indulged within their subconscious underdevelopment, contributing to self-destructive behaviors.

The pursuit of the "American Dream" creates a racial imbalance for Black people in achieving this objective. The "pull yourself up by our bootstraps" ideology is an all too true scenario of the Black reality, representing "cognitive dissonance" on a mainstream level. American culture exists as a fight to the death of individual and collective ascension that alters the sensitivity of the moral compass, negatively expanding the perceptive parameters of cruel and unusual justification. The symbolic ladder of social mobility of which Black America possesses the most obstructive climb of cultural elevation demonstrates the Malcolm X mentality "make it plain" of the racist Eugenics mantra "survival of the fittest" to exterminate Black people. Thus, the ideological "American Dream" as a form of achievement leads to the decline of Black mobility. The perceived reality of a racist and genocidal culture that spouts rhetoric from the pages of "sacred documents" penned by the torturous rapist and murderers of our ancestors and who would seek to invoke a process of conditioning that the Black collective remains unaware, basking within the slumber of the "American Dream" as the real-life nightmare is preyed upon, from the pulpit of a misguided and intellectually subjugated cultural dynamic.

Many Black people remain conditioned to the pathological misdirection of the "American Dream." The noble suffering of Black people is less impressive due to the directional instability of our corrective strategy to negate or transcend itself beyond its current condition. Our inner struggle to seek a reward for life by way of death remains the psychological allegory of our spiritual perception. The suppression of rage quakes within our deeper selves and manifests into self-destructive behaviors. One of those behaviors is the act of cultural assimilation, a product of White supremacy that perpetuates racial conflict. An inferiority complex from which many Black people suffer is detrimental to our cultural development, allowing racist ideology to dictate and surmise the conscious levels of our spiritual, psychological, and sociological condition.

White supremacists' social behaviors enhance the humanistic degradation of an entire culture.

While contentious berating and low-level conditioning are catalytic to individual and collective defense mechanisms, it also curtails constructive mediation. While Black people are not inherently culturally inferior, the psychological effects of racism can lead to cultural inferiority or self-hatred which negatively impacts our cultural Deoxyribonucleic Acid (DNA) across generations. This genocidal self-maintenance and psychological engineering is the invisible barrier obstructing cultural and racial unification. The internal war within a covert inner struggle maintains White racial superiority. When Black people are out of sync with their God-self, we take on a pseudo-culture of subservience that disrupts the developmental momentum and foundational stability critical to our cultural elevation.

Regardless of the individual or collective consciousness of the human endeavor, positive self-affirmation is foundational to any person or culture. The developmental ascension of our cultural reality that reprograms our knowledge of self is a tactic leading to the detriment of Black America; surviving as a subculture within our communities and void of ambitions to formulate a rising generational legacy. Perceptive expressions of free thought and free will are deceptive strategies of White supremacy leading to a host of reactive consequences that are both its poison and its antidote for the Black collective. The psychological duality of the "Massa... We Sick"? Syndrome exposes the incredulous progression of our condition as the more subservient Black leadership impedes upon a racist and oppressive hierarchy to "Save us from ourselves," further demonstrating the extent of our cultural psychosis leading us to live behind a well-practiced smile.

Powerful messages of revolutionary thought challenge a racist social order of control as a method to divide and constrict the structural mobility of our independent and unified elevation. Thus, initiatives of subversive strategies are integrated into the collective thoughts of the warrior psyche, inspired by a revolutionary rage against a morally conflicted and culturally suppressed reality. The contrasting submissive and aggressive persona depicted within our developmental behavioral patterns provides the necessary temperance and survivalism that inspires the adaptive consciousness to conceal real life behind a mask of hidden rage.

Imagine the coping mechanisms of a culture trapped within the genocidal realities of Slavery, Reconstruction, Jim Crow, and the Civil Rights era. Imagine, resisting the call of insanity- as your wife, husband, son, or daughter are forcibly gang raped, castrated, and murdered at the diabolical whim of a racist cultural ideology. Enduring the excruciating pain of being experimented upon, literally sliced open and dissected. Seeing your family and children bid upon and dehumanized at the auction block and literally sold down the river never to be seen again. Awakening to the stench of burning flesh as your loved ones tortured and lifeless bodies swing from the branches of the poplar trees or are left hanging from the massive, manufactured railroad overpasses. Controlling the deafening scream of fear and rage of seeing a strong Black man stripped naked, castrated, tarred, feathered, beaten to near death, set on fire, strapped to horses running in opposite directions, and literally torn apart. White supremacy dares to conceptualize and enact these torturous and humiliating events that are forever embedded in a traumatized matrix of our emotional and psychological processes. These are all acts of dehumanization and continuous factors of social and cultural conditioning currently implemented by the racist and class-defined ideology of American sociology.

Conditioned dependency is rooted in fear and humiliation residing within the formative processes of psychogenic and behavioral engineering, controlling the emotional variance of an entire culture.

Systems of control are relative to social and cultural events and influential to the structural reality of our condition. These systems of control strategically maintain the most profound conditions of cultural fear and intellectual subservience within the reactionary psyche of Black people. The perversely ambitious efforts of White supremacists to sustain our collective divisiveness is a racist construct that desperately embraces one of their greatest fears: the unification of Black people. White supremacists, quivering within the reality of their fear and cultural insecurity, anticipate the conscious rise of a tortured and long-sleeping culture. White supremacists have devised a strategy to eradicate the connection within our forgotten warrior self, inducing the spiritual and psychological amnesia of Black genius. This amnesia strategically mutes Black perception to see no farther than the confines of a fixed environment which is essential to establishing the permanence of the oppressive state.

Our "dog eat dog" mentality is the way in which we adapt to the harsh terrain of the Black social reality. This deliberate incursion of cultural and social dysfunction interjected into the interactive mechanics of our character and behavior skews our perception and distorts our ability to determine the real enemy and oppressor. Perceptions of success and satisfaction for Black people in America fit into a compressed reality too small for the ambitions of an entire culture. There is no room for creative and structural ideology to be constructed and processed. Contumacious reactions become cultural norms, testing emotional frustrations and social discontent.

There is a conscious realization of our inability to decipher and reconstruct a dilemma that is contentious to the social and emotional order of the culture that inhibits the catalyst of individual and collective motivation necessary for the unification and manifestation of Black power. This epiphanic search for the inspiration of the enlightenment is prophetic to the reality of our suppressed and hidden rage.

We have spoken into existence the manifestation of our lesser selves. The perpetuation of subservience detrimentally regulates cultural progression, contributing to a weakened resistance, as the instinctive "go-along to get-along" lifestyle benefits White supremacy. This skewed sense of social mobility systematically unbalances the scales of conscious morality, influencing a distorted moral and social construct within a person. From "My Brother" to "My Nigga" from "My Queen" to "My Bitch" demonstrates the impact of subliminal messaging negatively influencing Black people's self-perception. Black people's poor self-perception is a structural cornerstone of White supremacy that curtails ascension.

While simplistic in concept and structure, White supremacy is not to be underestimated. Social manipulation influences self-perception and is instrumental in the psychological maintenance of the Black mind. Cultural control enacts and sustains the self-incriminating mechanisms that thwart individual and collective development. Behavioral triggers are influential determinants that manifest the productive value of our reality. The dismantling of human dignity, self-preservation, and cultural awareness is most effective in our sociological and psychological imaging that has negatively affected an entire culture. Essentially, spiritual exploration is necessary to stretch beyond the terroristic and subversive indoctrinations of White supremacy.

The vestiges of self-hatred and the innate fear of the suppressive and genocidal wrath of White supremacy is a tool of psychological weaponry that alters the developmental trajectory of our reality. Its effects are as a contagion, derived from a sickness that originated from yet a greater sickness that remains instilled within the complex processes of our character. These debilitating conditions that compromise the mechanics of creative and intellectual thought are elements uniquely essential to the structural stability that sustains the greatness and longevity of any culture.

This identity crisis is not to be underestimated. The effects are far-reaching, perpetuating racial conflict, especially intercultural conflict undermining the cohesiveness of the global Black community.

The strategic initiatives that contribute to the stagnation of Black growth and development are significant to the incursion of Black-on-Black conflict and debilitation.

Ironically our misfortune is a financial funding source for White supremacist industrialists by way of the *Three Strike Laws, The War on Drugs, and the No Child Left Behind Act.*

These pseudo-political outreaches masquerade as initiatives of social justice and change.

Many of our cultural interactions– expressed through contention, confrontation, and disrespect– are foundational within our culture and fractured by the stresses of self-hatred and learned helplessness. Racist misconceptions derived from the divisive conditioning of White supremacy connect to the spiritual identity of the Black collective, which complicates and misrepresents the Black culture leading to the unimaginable genocide of countless generations.

As Black America awaits an epiphany of developmental enlightenment, White supremacy remains within the demented convictions of racial and cultural superiority that would concede to any sociological event of applied dehumanization. As a result, genetic mobility begins and arrives at the same place within the conscious stagnation of its continuity and remains a convincing illusion of our individual and cultural elevation. This inevitably suppresses the perceptive ambitions of a generation.

Our conflicted mindset and behaviors reflect the success of White supremacy as it has led to cultural conditioning and psychological control in the Black community. Progressive thinking across generations is required to better unify the Black collective. The rise of spiritual and cultural awareness aims to re-design the sociological terrain of a racist and sadistic existence of subservience and oppression. Cultural cognizance relating to the evaluation of value systems remains misrepresented and misleading to racial and social mobility.

White supremacy creates and perpetuates stereotypes reflecting the stark reality of cultural deficiency, leading to internal hatred, thus, a misdirection of consciousness, leading to dire consequences. The reality is that we are living in warzones, but we must rise as a whole system that is pitted against us not only by racism but by psychological oppression. Black people are boiling over as they exist within the muffled considerations of their imagination, quietly simmering beneath the reality of their suppressed and hidden rage.

There is a contentious reaction to circumstantial events that manipulate the structures of our character and influence the determinants of cultural perception that impact the eventual outcomes and consequences of our reality. These outcomes and consequences are often determined by the reactive instincts of our perspective capabilities that weigh upon the balances of deciding our oppression or our liberation. Our innate fear of confronting our spiritual, psychological, and cultural dehumanization creates aggression, self-hate, and conflict. Subconscious stagnation has psychologically restricted elevational thought. This continued regression of the higher levels of ourselves has left us subjected to the spiritual and mental reconstruction of the psychotic and sociopathic tactics of White supremacy.

It is sometimes within the unpronounced and clandestine realities of fear that would unfurl the psychotic and genocidal wrath upon another culture, greater than itself.

The uncompromising condition of reality transcends the most basic concepts of morality to defy the most common mutuality of humanistic preservation.

There is a meditative process that inhibits both, the calculated and spontaneous processes of anger; confronting the power of our inner selves that would explore the higher accesses of discretionary consciousness, that would contemplate upon the justices and injustices of applied confrontation.

The skewed tactical mindset of the Black collective operates within the framework of perceptive and strategic misdirection. This psychological reversal of thought that creates and perpetuates the real-life confrontation of the enemy not only distracts from but rearranges the basic ideological constructs of cultural responsibility and action, as the adverse totality of sociological destruction remains indelible within the creative and productive spaces that exist within the complex framework of behavioral and social control.

The diabolical construct of White supremacy incites the consciousness of a deep contemplation from fear to rage.

It is within the trembling hopes of the oppressor that this rage of the enlightened is tempered with the transcendent morality of spirituality, more so than the primal and aggressive reflexes of humanistic justification.

The sociological and psychological status quo imposed upon the Black collective by the White supremacist construct is now being challenged and aggressively rejected.

From beneath the veil of social conditioning of Black people, the obstruction of our oppression transcends the conscious perceptions of our liberation. The determination to remain uncompromising and unapologetic is an essential element to the collective elevation of any culture.

Passive resistance and other nebulous concepts of morality may prove meritless when contemplating mental, spiritual, and physical warfare.

There are aspects of a culture that reflect its social and moral standing. However, the effects of suppression ultimately diminish progressive thought and self-determination. For example, the concept of hope is a programming strategy, a deviously orchestrated ideological and subversive control tactic utilized to influence the spiritual and psychological chain of events that would breathe life into the legacy of a once subservient culture reflective of a conditioned psychosis.

Despite the decimation of cultural compassion and morality, a spiritual connection between the individual and collective is essential to the survival and elevation of any culture. Our learning process exists within repressive constraints that deny creativity and criticality to re-establish human contemplation and moralistic control.

The spirit's true capabilities are compromised, leading to the impersonation of the oppressor. The individual and collective falter within the blinding glare of elevational probability. The subconscious obstruction of creative discovery distorts clarity and vision, perpetuating the adversarial conditions that strengthen White supremacy.

The Black community's search for justice is fundamentally flawed. The "I hate you because you're so much like me" perceptions of self are deceptively valid within our interactions. It's also within the context of our progressive separation that heavily plays upon the probabilities of our independent and cultural elevation. Because we hate the reality of our reflective selves, we are just as vicious of the consciously emboldened self who dares to resist conformity, stepping outside the proverbial "box."

Compromised integrity speaks to a culture that finds its comfort zone within a skewed and idealistically reversed perception of its own demise. When the permanence of behavioral deterioration becomes more common within the normalcy of our culture, our proverbial "comfort zone" begins to counteract our oppression. As frustration, anger, and self-hatred grow, the concepts of individual and cultural expansion derived from our ancestors fade from our memory.

Due to our low expectations of self, we subconsciously falter within the creation of our levels of structural empowerment and relinquish control for fear of confronting our humanistic and spiritual individuality. We magnify our hidden idiosyncrasies into collective and individual dysfunction. This self-deception justifies blame and diminishes any responsibility imposed upon us by White supremacy. This epiphany would then call upon the rages of our oppression to test the transcendent powers of our spiritual and conscious elevation, extending beyond our current condition of conformity to cultural and social norms. What of the learned behavior of a people whose critical rationale remains of psychological and spiritual manipulation to surrender their unified power of creative and implemental control to languish within the perverse reality of the twisted and horrific images of their greatest adversary?

The influence of an insidious regime leaves scars upon a shaken and unconscious culture in quest of its lost identity. The conditions of righteousness and the realization of inner greatness are compromised to project a reflective image of a superficial mentality that corrupts spirituality and diminishes the contemplation of thought. There is no proverbial "window of opportunity" for those whose lack of vision to conceive of an expansion beyond their condition would underestimate the untapped potential and power of their greater self to relinquish the unspent anger of justifiable reason unto the sick and genocidal devices of White supremacy.

Testing the volume of our trepidation as an ironic catalyst of our innate survival instincts is essential to the subversive influences that attempt to infiltrate the unified core of the Black collective that are divisive to the positive perception and mobility of our culture.

The continuity of our spiritual and psychological stability teeters upon a precipice of conceptual self-hatred, evoking a psychological fear that would turn the other cheek from the megalomania of diabolical human experimentation and sociological engineering. This invasive process of counter-cultural indoctrination diminishes the original self and alters the basic concepts of spirituality and self-empowerment to contaminate the purpose and mission of Black power. Our stunted vision cannot see beyond the confines of immediacy and strives only to the lower reaches of tailored conditions that would denounce the rebellious voices of those cultural and generational warriors.

Addressing the self before engaging the terroristic and genocidal realities of a dreaded mortal enemy is in the greater interest of collective unity. This strategy directly addresses conflict. A new sense of enlightenment makes plain the abstract perceptions that are conceptually blinded within its manipulation of psychological conditioning that would touch upon a wave of unknown anger.

By what measure is the consideration of rebellion; not only against the systematic and psychological infestation of White supremacy but of the spiritual and cultural struggle within us that compromises our completeness? Infiltrators who need not the cover of darkness to gain closeness and ways of access. The perfection of their perpetration is at ease, as they are natural to the presence of their prey.

Our tenuous interjection into the conventional cultural dynamics of our society is one of a selective immersion into the White mainstream, as opposed to a more external expression of sociological independence and conscious elevation. The psychological tools of an enemy are far more dangerous. For their mask is not a mask at all. Furthermore, if the value of freedom requires sacrifice, what becomes of the person detached from their spiritual self as a loyalist to the sadistic and immoral ethics of an adversary?

Those who are from us, but not of us, must not be considered unfortunate casualties of cultural and generational warfare and are active participants in this real-life conflict in which the commonality of death is a standardized actuality within the lives of Black men, women, and children.

We must examine the "power bases" within Black America. For example, influencers who sit in the seats of authority in our culture and clinch their fist in symbolic gestures of Black power but are covert tacticians and strategists who inspire and initiate the mechanisms of our collective subservience before the rest of the world.

The moralistic hypocrisy within the corrupt and pervasive arenas of religion and politics; dope dealers and killers who are blind loyalists, claiming the identification and possession of streets and neighborhoods that are not their own; community activists and organizations who take government payoffs and sell out the hopes and the futures of our children within the guise of weak "conflict resolution" and "cultural diversity" programs. The reconstruction or the eradication of these systems of our demise must be taken under deep consideration, as the tedious viability toward transcending these adversarial conditions is changing the perpetual cycle of repetition into the permanence of concrete reality. The repetition of our actions as they relate to the vicious cycle of our discontent plays out within both fixed and conflicting thoughts.

This psychological rationale that concedes to a desire to remain as we currently are causes concern and re-evaluation to determine the levels of our stagnation that indoctrinate us into the mimicry and suppressive ideology of White supremacy.

Revolutionary consciousness is necessary when contemplating the strategies of war. The integrity of any culture depends upon the structural competence of its combined thought and implemental intent that would elevate and make plain the conceptual dynamics and objective complexities of warfare, waged upon both the subconscious and conscious levels from the psychological, spiritual, and physical plateaus of the altercation.

The realization and the acquisition of power should be among our primary and committed levels of focus. From the most basic and foundational levels of concentrated thought and action, the initiative to seize control of our personal space and sociological environments is necessary for our cultural elevation. So reversed within the logic of self-preservation, we would vanquish ourselves rather than oppose the architects and the ominous caretakers of our diminished capacities.

Many elders in the Black community show their disgust and disdain for the "demonstrative" rages of the youth. They often struggle to realize it is within their oppressed fear of confrontation that they would erroneously scapegoat their misguided perceptions onto the already emotionally unstable realities of our children. Our failure to realize our psychosis is the stagnating element detaining our conscious and cultural elevation.

A psychological and physical uprising, if you will, speaks to the familiarity of an abandoned consciousness that hides within the recesses of our volatility and steps unsure into the inevitable confrontation with not only the contentious objectives of White supremacy but into the spiritual and psychological liberation of the subjugated.

Our physical and psychological desecration of Black power speaks to the familiarity of a condition controlled by fear and maintained by the conditional influences of behavioral repetition. There is a proverbial, close-ended loop that denies the ability to perpetuate potential and makes realistic the perceptive blockade to visualize our individual and collective elevation.

The vast underestimation, or intentional denial of the inner genetic modification that has altered the structural masses of our psychological and emotional character, are conditionally transfixed within the tenuous development of our evolution. It is only through that of which we have been told is forbidden thought; that we would conquer and transcend the purveyor of our captivity.

The non-verbal expression of the rebellious voice that strains itself within the rumbling volatility of its silence is reactive to a fit of anger that is conceptually inconceivable from any level of the demented imagination of White supremacists.

The stressors of White supremacy inhibit the independent thinking of the Black individual and collective. These factors are relevant to the basic construct of action and reaction, as they pertain to the unbalanced logistics of forgiveness versus retribution.

What of a perverse mortal enemy on an erroneous search for honor, whereas it is known, even unto themselves, that they are inherently dishonorable? That who would instead recalibrate the logistic and the conscious reality of a moral compass that is more compatible with the twisted framework of their own fragmented and demented ideology.

Our conscious indecision of the fight or flight mentality maintains the developmental mediocrity and the mundane currency of our dilemma that stagnates the humanistic exploration of spiritual and psychological evolution.

It is within the tenuous embrace of our own insecurity that speaks to the fragility of our potential to excel beyond the confines of our own psychosis, as we would proceed to be willing participants of an oppressive ideology that maintains the abhorrent networks of a suppressive and stagnating structural template of reality.

Our conscious realization of the unfamiliar instruments afforded to us by the tenants of a demented counterculture, in effect, are emotional and psychological tools utilized to compromise and make submissive the most basic constructs of rebellion.

There is a cognitive slumber that stagnates the constructive evolution of human potential and creates a cycle of self-deprivation that creates the clouded perceptive reasonings of an inferior identity.

Our inability to recognize intellectual warfare and its manipulation mislead the radicalized masses, causing them to conform to a more submissive mindset of passive-resistant entrapment.

This hostile takeover of the mind and spirit has led to many in the Black community to embody submissive standards of the oppressive state. This psychological hijack inspires the need to eradicate White supremacy as a culture and a system. Understanding this reality is the first step to activating catalytic change. The truth living deep within the soul of the conqueror is unapologetic. For it is this person who is the administrator and the purveyor of justice or injustice.

The rebellious voice within us must serve to condemn the twisted desires of a demented mortal enemy and obliterate the motivator of its torment. Our steps must be bold and potentially explosive to transcend our current levels of "action" and "reaction." It is within the conditioned restraint of our mind that we must rise above any inferiority complex dwelling deep within us and elevate beyond the familiar confines of its repetition.

Essentially, there is a need for a unified collective of Black people to share the same ideology and goals in establishing a progressive legacy for future generations.

Seeking the voices of a movement of people captivates and transforms the stagnation of incoherent rhetoric into active determination and rebelliously shakes the structural foundation of the oppressive state.

Our incapability to expand beyond the currency of our environment is contagious to the elemental suppression of free thought and free will. This incapability holds hostage to our developmental probability that would conquer and eradicate the psychological element of our oppression.

Black America's national protest of race, class, and cultural terrorism is a method of manipulation by White supremacists. The deceptive intent projecting racist Americans as caring about and listening to the concerns of Black people demonstrates the hypocrisy of the "American Dream."

Like the Jewish community that has garnered cultural empowerment and worldwide support for their mantra "Never Again" in protest and solidarity against the heinous acts of the holocaust. "Black Power" is a cultural mantra of self-empowerment, pride, and protest of Black people in America.

Fleeting inspiration through racial and social justice trends are the rhythmic chants and mantras of the Black collective, such as "Black Lives Matter" and "No Justice, No Peace," is a conscious effort to appeal to the deceptive morality of White supremacy. These loud and clear messages demonstrate to the world the racist realities of a sick and sadistic society. However, these messages are not always received by those it's against as expected.

The expectations that social justice and equal opportunity are applicable because they are righteous in "the cause" are the perceptive pipedreams of the oppressed masses. The current content of social functionality speaks to the elemental core of our dilemma and eliminates all factors of probability and doubt that question the subversive manifestation of our reality in real-time.

To be Black and to speak of "Black Power" would give cause to the supremacist political hierarchy to create and initiate racist and suppressive methods of control, such as COINTELPRO (Counterintelligence Program) and BIE (Black Identity Extremist) to monitor Black cultural thought and action processes in the prevention of, as J. Edgar Hoover, Former Director of the Federal Bureau of Investigation (FBI), once described as "The Rise of a Black Messiah."

The psychological conditioning of our cultural morality exists as a complex and dangerous concept as it triggers a reactive response from Black people to justify their dehumanization and life suffering as a "God send." This justification tests the balance of faith and spiritual commitment, which is egregiously self-serving to the racist and demented agenda of White supremacists.

White racists are intimidated by Black people's intrinsic brilliance. Any inclination of Black strength on any level leads to fear and trepidation among White supremacists. This emotional response speaks to how racism is enacted through subjugation and oppression, leading to spiritual and psychological warfare against Black people. These conditions profoundly shape the basic structures of social and cultural events through stimuli pertaining to ambition, family structure, community, and spiritual values.

The most common response of the oppressed masses often results in "protest marches" and "prayer vigils." While therapeutic and reactionary to some degree, these emotional outbursts, unfortunately, pacify aggression and maintain the psychological and spiritual slumber of the more progressive and radical Black consciousness dynamic.

It is at the developmental conception of our most simplistic selves that stands at the summit of our knowledge--whispering metaphorically-- to awaken the revolutionary consciousness of our culture. From the smallest of inferences to the most powerful heights of our own self-perception, our awakening begins at our introduction of self. This re-shaping process signifies the spiritually and psychologically distorted version of ourselves imposed upon us by the ways of ignorance and was utilized in vain to manipulate our cultural chemistry that would subversively diminish the boundless creativity and brilliance of Black power.

BOOK DISCUSSION QUESTIONS

1. How would you define White supremacy?

2. Who is responsible for enacting the tenets of White supremacy?

3. Describe the effects of psychological conditioning on an individual and collective level.

4. What is the meaning of the *title Hostile Takeover: A Systematic and Psychological Manifestation of a Cultural Reality*?

5. What aspect of the book was most impactful, if any?

6. What are the foundational contributors to racial oppression?

7. After reading the book:

   a. What is your perception of racial conflict in America?

   b. What is your final summation of *Hostile Takeover*?

ABOUT THE AUTHOR

 Duane Campbell, a native of Buffalo, New York, and transplant to Louisville, Kentucky, is the son of now-deceased parents and the youngest of three brothers. Campbell graduated from Central High School. He is also a proud veteran of the United States Army. While pursuing a college degree, he took two years of courses specializing in sociology and psychology. Campbell's poetic writing style fuses a rhythmic cadence that is sometimes rule-breaking in its grammatical nuisances and represents his expressive identity. Now, as an accomplished author, Campbell's writing is inspired by the work of authors, including his late father Ralph A. Campbell, as well as Malcolm X, Dr. Frances Cress Welsing, Kahlil Gibran, Steve Coakley, James Baldwin, Dr. Amos Wilson, Fred Hampton, Baba Dr. John Henrik Clarke, and Baba Dick Gregory. Over the years, Campbell has served as a motivational speaker and lecturer across the country in diverse settings. He is the author of more than three books and resides in Louisville, Kentucky.

Milton Keynes UK
Ingram Content Group UK Ltd.
UKHW020655191023
430917UK00014B/430

9 798987 833612